Just 21 Days

112211

OrangeBooks Publication

1st Floor, Rajhans Arcade, Mall Road, Kohka, Bhilai, Chhattisgarh 490020

Website: **www.orangebooks.in**

First Edition, 2025

ISBN: 978-93-6554-165-6

Price: Rs. 449.00

Printed in India

JUST 21 DAYS

That's all it takes

To Manifest Your Most Burning Desire

With Gratitude
Nisha Jain

A Sacred Manifestation Journey Through Vedic Teachings, Energy Rituals, and the Law of Attraction.

Dedication

To the one holding this book right now...
To the part of you that's still showing up – even with tears in your eyes and hope flickering inside.
To the woman or man who's heard "not enough" too many times...
To the mother doing her best every single day...
To the seeker waking up at 4:30 AM – not just to rise, but to remember...
This book is for you.

For the version of me – Nisha – who once felt lost, overwhelmed, and unsure if she would ever feel whole again.
And for the version of you that's now ready to say:
"No more surviving. I choose to thrive."

With all my heart,
Nisha Jain

Gentle Disclaimer

With deep gratitude, I offer this book as a companion on your journey – not as a prescription, but as an invitation.

The stories, rituals, and practices shared here come from my own research, sunrise disciplines, Vedic wisdom, and lived experiences. They are meant to inspire, guide, and awaken – but your path is uniquely yours.

I am not a medical, psychological, or legal professional, and this book is not a replacement for professional advice. If you have health concerns – physical or emotional – please seek guidance from a qualified expert alongside your practice here.

Your results will be as unique as your fingerprint. Some shifts may be subtle, others profound. Trust your pace. Trust your timing. Trust the Universe's way of delivering what's meant for you.

As you walk through these 21 days, may you carry this knowing in your heart:

You are your own greatest guide, and the magic was always within you.

Table of Contents

Table of Contents

Table of Contents

Gratitude & Acknowledgements

Gratitude is the soul of this book. It's where everything begins – and ends.

To the Universe – thank you for every divine detour, every delay that was really protection, and every soul encounter that shaped me. You led me even when I didn't see the path.

To the angels in my life – in spirit, in strangers, in dreams – thank you for showing up exactly when I needed you, often without even knowing I did. You reminded me:

I am never alone.

I am always guided.

I am always loved.

To my Maa – my grandmother. You were the first divine feminine in my life. Quiet, powerful, and always present. Your blessings still wrap around me like sacred protection.

To my Jisa – my grandfather, my first mentor. You didn't just raise me – you shaped me.

When I was a little girl, you once said, "Never ask or borrow. If you want something, create it."

That sentence rewired my soul.

You were wealthy beyond measure but lived humbly. You gifted me more than abundance – you gave me a mindset.

To my Maasa – your prayers are my invisible armour. Your love flows like a sacred river. You are my reminder of unspoken, divine connection.

Gratitude & Acknowledgements

To my daughter, Pia — my reason, my rhythm, my reflection. You have seen me break, rise, and rebuild. You are proof that a woman can rise and raise — with love, power, and grace.

To my family and friends — thank you for the support, the silence, the distance, and the closeness. It all shaped me.

To my clients, my soul circle, and my mentors — you've been part of my expansion. Thank you for trusting me, for showing up, and for walking this journey with me.

To the strangers — the cab driver who waited, the friend who became family, the podcast host I've never met — thank you.

And lastly, to the younger version of me:

The girl who cried in silence. Who woke at 4:30 AM just to keep trying.

I see you. I honour you. We made it.

This book is a love letter to you — and to every soul holding on with invisible thread and unshakable spirit.

With peace in my heart and fire in my soul.

About the Author

I'm Nisha Jain – a simple woman, a mother, and a soul seeker just like you.

There was a time when I felt lost, unsure, and deeply alone on my path. No mentors, no map – only a quiet fire inside me that said, keep going.

Through years of 4:30 AM rituals, silent tears, tapping, prayer, and presence, I began to remember who I was.

I didn't write this book because I had everything figured out.

I wrote it because I stopped waiting to be ready – and chose to show up anyway.

This is for every soul whispering, "There must be more."

There is. It begins inside you.

Welcome home to your becoming.

Nisha Jain

Introduction: Why This Book Was Born

This book wasn't planned. It was prayed.

Born from my deepest breakdowns and the quietest mornings where I sat cross-legged in silence and asked the Universe: "What now?"

As a woman and a mother with no support system, I had two choices: to break down... or to rise and build myself stronger than ever.

So, I began waking early – not to hustle, but to align.

I tapped. I visualised. I cried. I gave thanks.

I remembered.

Slowly, my energy shifted. My life transformed.

People asked what changed – and I'd say:

"I don't chase. I align."

This book is that alignment – in 21 days.

It brings together ancient Vedic wisdom, energy rituals, EFT tapping, and the Law of Attraction into a gentle daily rhythm.

It's not about being perfect.

It's about being present.

This book is your sunrise, your map, your mirror.

And I'll walk with you – every step.

Good News: You've Already Begun

The moment you picked up this book, something shifted.
You're not starting from scratch – You're starting from spirit.
Every page ahead is here to help you remember what your soul already knows.
Your desire is sacred.
Your energy is magnetic.
And your daily practice is how you align them.
This isn't just a book.
It's a 21-day energetic reset – a sacred invitation to rise.
If you show up...
The Universe will meet you.

The Power of Vedic Wisdom, Energy Rituals & the Law of Attraction

I've always been drawn to Vedic stories. There's a deep energy in them – not just as tales from the past, but as powerful metaphors for our lives today.

At the same time, I've worked with modern tools like the Law of Attraction, EFT tapping, affirmations, and visualisations.

And I realised: they aren't different paths. They're all part of the same sacred truth – your energy creates your reality.

When we combine these powerful tools – ancient stories that speak to the soul and modern energy techniques that shift our nervous system – the results are magical.

This book is where East meets West. Spirit meets science. Story meets energy. And your life begins to change from the inside out.

How to Use This Book

This isn't something you just read.
It's something you live.

Each of the 21 days includes:

1. Vedic Teaching or Archetype

Stories from ancient texts – simplified and spiritual. You'll meet Arjuna, Hanuman, Maitreyi, and others. These aren't just stories – they reflect parts of you.

2. Law of Attraction Insight

Each day brings an energy lesson:

- Embodying gratitude
- Detaching from outcome
- Becoming a vibrational match

This is how you attract – not from need, but from alignment.

How to Use This Book

3. EFT Tapping – How to Use This Ritual

EFT stands for Emotional Freedom Technique. It's a simple but powerful way to release resistance, clear emotional blocks, and raise your vibration.

Here's how you do it:

➤ Step 1: Acknowledge how you feel
Start by tapping and saying what you're honestly feeling. Example: "Even though I feel doubtful or scared, I deeply and completely love and accept myself."

➤ Step 2: Tap on these 9 meridian points while repeating affirmations:

1. Karate Chop Point (side of the hand)
2. Top of the Head
3. Eyebrow Point
4. Side of the Eye
5. Under the Eye
6. Under the Nose
7. Chin
8. Collarbone
9. Under the Arm

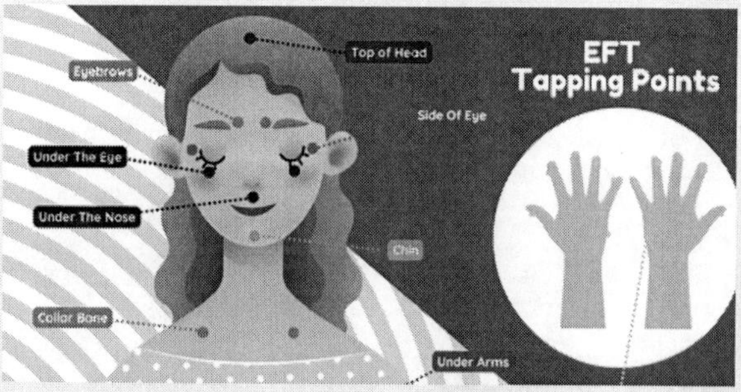

Gently tap each point 5–7 times while speaking positive affirmations or the truth you're processing.
You'll feel lighter, more centered, and deeply connected. You can't do this wrong – just follow your breath and let your energy shift.

How to Use This Book

4. Letter to the Universe

Each day, you'll write from the end result, as if it's already done. This builds trust, faith, and connection with your higher self.

5. Intention Box Prompt

Write your intention (as if it's already real) and place it in a journal or intention box. This is how we plant energetic seeds.

6. Journaling Reflection

Track your energy, emotions, clarity, and progress. You'll be amazed how much can shift in 21 days.

You don't have to do it perfectly.

You just need to show up.

Final Words Before You Begin

You don't need to have it all figured out.

You don't need to be perfect.

You just need to be present.

Light a candle.

Open your heart.

And let these 21 days guide you back to your truth.

Because the real manifestation... is you becoming you again.

With sunrise love,

Nisha Jain

Day 1: Arjuna's Collapse – Detachment from Outcome

Theme: "Do your dharma. Let go of the fruit."

Arjuna on the Battlefield

The battlefield of Kurukshetra trembled with silence. Dust hung in the air. Horses neighed. Conches blew. Yet in the middle of this grand war stood Arjuna, the greatest archer of his time, paralysed – not with fear, but with emotion.

He saw his teachers, his cousins, his friends – all on the other side of the battlefield. These were not just enemies; they were parts of his life. His arms weakened. His bow slipped from his hand. His warrior's heart questioned everything.

"How can I kill those I love? What victory is worth this sacrifice? If I win, what is left of joy? If I lose, what is left of honor?"

And right beside him sat Krishna, not just his charioteer, but the Divine in human form – calm, unwavering.

Krishna did not push him. He did not shame his doubt.

He whispered a truth that would shake the foundation of every seeker for millennia:

"You have the right to your actions, but never to the fruits of those actions."

(Bhagavad Gita – 2.47)

He continued:

"Act, Arjuna, not out of fear or desire. Do what is yours to do – and let go of what is not yours to control."

That one sentence pierced the fog in Arjuna's mind. He did not suddenly feel fearless, but he felt clear. He picked up his bow again not to fight for victory, but to fight for alignment.

Law of Attraction Insight:

Do the Work – Then Let It Go

- **The Universe doesn't respond to pressure.**
- **It responds to energy – calm, clear, committed.**
- **When you take action from desperation, you signal a lack.**
- **When you take action with trust, you become magnetic.**

The detachment Krishna taught isn't indifference – it's sacred surrender. It's knowing that your job is the aligned action. The Universe's job is the outcome.

Daily Soul Practice

1. Write Your Most Burning Desire

Be honest. What is your soul truly asking for? Write it clearly, without hesitation.

My most burning desire is:

....
....
....
....
....
....
....
....
....
....
....
....
....
....
....
....
....
....
....
....

2. EFT Tapping Script (Repeat 3 Rounds)

Karate Chop Point:
"Even though I feel anxious about the outcome, I deeply and completely love and accept myself."

Eyebrow: I'm ready to release control

Side of Eye: I've been holding on too tightly

Under Eye: I trust that my aligned action is enough

Under Nose: I let go of needing to control results

Chin: I act from purpose, not fear

Collarbone: I am guided by something greater

Under Arm: The Universe is handling the how

Top of Head: I surrender the outcome with peace

Take 3 deep breaths. Drink some water.

3. Letter to the Universe

Dear Universe,

Today, I choose action that aligns with my truth.
I trust you to carry my offerings forward.
I release the need to control or force what's next.
I trust in divine timing, and I know that my work is enough.
Thank you for walking this path with me.
It is already done.

With love,
[Your Name]

4. Intention Box Prompt

"Today, I acted in alignment. I release control. I invite peace."
Write it. Feel it. Place it in your journal or intention box:

5. Journal Reflection

- **What action did I take today from alignment?**
- **Where did I feel resistance?**
- **What did the tapping bring up?**
- **What emotions did I release?**

Reflection:

Day 1: Arjuna's Collapse – Detachment from Outcome

Theme: "Do your dharma. Let go of the fruit."

Energy Summary

Before: Overthinking, fear, control
After: Peace, clarity, aligned power
Like Arjuna, your power lies not in controlling the outcome – but in honouring your path.
You are not here to force. You are here to offer.
Let today be your bow to the Divine.

Day 2: Hanuman – Identity Attracts, Not Effort

Theme: "Your power isn't something to earn.
It's something to remember."

Hanuman's Leap Across the Ocean

There was a moment when the Vanara army stood stuck at the edge of a vast ocean.

They had found Sita's whereabouts – trapped across the sea in Lanka. But no one knew how to get there.

And then someone turned to Hanuman.

"Can you leap?" they asked.

Hanuman looked at the endless blue before him and... hesitated.

He had forgotten.

He had forgotten that he was divine – the son of the Wind God, the embodiment of Shiva's energy.

He had forgotten that he had once swallowed the sun as a child.

He had forgotten the power that lived in his very breath.

That's when Jambavan, the wise elder, stepped forward.

He didn't teach Hanuman new skills. He didn't hand him new weapons.

He simply reminded him:

"You already have the power. You've always had it."

And in that moment – something clicked.

Hanuman stood taller. His energy surged.

He remembered.

And with a single leap, he soared across the ocean, into history, into legend.

Law of Attraction Insight:

Identity Attracts. Not Just Action.

We don't manifest what we work hard for.

We manifest what we believe we already are.

Hanuman's power didn't come from training.

It came from awareness. From identity.

When you align your identity with the version of you who already has it, the Universe responds instantly.

The thoughts you think, the way you walk, speak, act – they all signal who you believe you are.

The shift isn't in trying harder.

The shift is in remembering who you already are.

Theme: "Your power isn't something to earn. It's something to remember."

Daily Soul Practice

1. Write Your Most Burning Desire

Write it not from need, but from your power.

My most burning desire is:

2. EFT Tapping Script (Repeat 3 Rounds)

Karate Chop Point:
"Even though I forgot my true power, I deeply and completely love and accept myself."

Eyebrow: I've been doubting my abilities

Side of Eye: I forgot who I am

Under Eye: But the power never left me

Under Nose: I am born of divine energy

Chin: I carry ancient strength within me

Collarbone: My breath is sacred. My energy is potent

Under Arm: I'm not here to earn worth – I AM it

Top of Head: I remember. I reclaim. I rise.

Take 3 deep breaths. Drink water.

3. Letter to the Universe

Dear Universe,
I am done pretending to be small.
I am ready to walk as my full self –
not the version chasing worth, but the one embodying it.
Remind me when I forget.
Catch me when I shrink.
Help me leap, like Hanuman, into my divine becoming.
Thank you for trusting me with this power.
I won't waste it.
With love,
[Your Name]

4. Intention Box Prompt

"I walk as the version of me who already has what I desire. I remember my true self."
Write it. Feel it. Drop it into your energetic vault:

5. Journal Reflection

- **Where have I been playing small?**
- **What identity am I ready to release?**
- **What does the version of me who has it think and feel like?**
- **What emotions surfaced during tapping?**

Reflection:

Day 2: Hanuman – Identity Attracts, Not Effort

Theme: "Your power isn't something to earn.
It's something to remember."

Energy Summary

Before: Doubt, forgetfulness, external validation

After: Power, remembrance, embodiment

Hanuman didn't need to become powerful.

He just needed to remember.

So do you.

Day 3: Rudraka – Gratitude Creates Reality

Theme: "What you thank, stays. What you notice, grows."

Rudraka's Return to the Forest

Rudraka was a forest-dwelling sage with very little in the material sense – no wealth, no power, no home in the cities. Yet kings came to him. Disciples bowed to him. Even the gods, it is said, watched him with reverence.

Why?

Because Rudraka radiated something rare – contentment.

When asked how he attracted so much without seeking anything, he simply said:

"My days begin and end in gratitude. And gratitude multiplies what I already have."

He gave thanks for his one meal, for the shade of a tree, for the breeze, for silence, for his breath.

He didn't wait for abundance to arrive before feeling abundant – he created abundance by feeling it in advance.

When a disciple once asked, "How do I receive more in life?"

Rudraka smiled and said,

"Begin with thanks. Because the Universe cannot resist a grateful heart."

Law of Attraction Insight:

Gratitude is Magnetic.
Every thought emits a frequency.
But gratitude emits one of the highest.
When you express thanks before the outcome...
You collapse timelines.
You signal trust.
You show the Universe that you're already a match to more.
So many of us wait for results to feel grateful.
But energy works backwards: when you feel it first, you receive it faster.
Don't wait. Start thanking. Now.

Daily Soul Practice

1. Write Your Most Burning Desire

But this time, write it with a tone of thanks — as if it's already happened.

My most burning desire is:

2. EFT Tapping Script (Repeat 3 Rounds)

Karate Chop Point:

"Even though I sometimes forget to feel grateful, I deeply and completely love and accept myself."

Eyebrow: I choose gratitude today

Side of Eye: I already have so much

Under Eye: I see beauty in the ordinary

Under Nose: I feel thankful before results

Chin: I trust life's timing

Collarbone: I welcome miracles with an open heart

Under Arm: The more I thank, the more I receive

Top of Head: My vibration is pure gratitude

Take 3 deep breaths. Drink water.

3. Intention Box Prompt

"Gratitude is my frequency. I receive through appreciation, not chasing."
Write and place it with intention:

4. Letter to the Universe

Dear Universe,

Thank you for what's here.

Thank you for what's on its way.

Thank you for everything I can't yet see but already trust.

I release neediness.

I welcome peace.

I say thank you with my full heart, because my life is already abundant.

And the rest? It's just icing.

With love,

(Your Name)

5. Journal Reflection

- **What am I deeply grateful for right now?**
- **How does gratitude shift my energy?**
- **Where can I appreciate more without waiting for change?**

Reflection:

Day 3: Rudraka – Gratitude Creates Reality

Theme: "What you thank, stays. What you notice, grows."

Energy Summary

Before: Lack, wanting, pressure

After: Fullness, receptivity, joy

Rudraka didn't wait for blessings to feel blessed.

And neither should you.

Start where you are. Say thank you – again and again.

And watch how the Universe says,

"Here's more."

Day 4: Shaileya – Embody Abundance First

Theme: "Live like Lakshmi already lives in your home."

Shaileya and the Visit of Lakshmi

In a small, unadorned hermitage deep in the forest lived a humble sage named Shaileya. Unlike other rishis who performed elaborate yagnas or sought spiritual powers, Shaileya's only daily ritual was silent devotion and hospitality.

He kept his hut clean, lit a diya every evening, arranged fresh flowers at the altar, and prepared food with love – as if a divine guest might arrive at any moment.

One day, the goddess Lakshmi herself appeared at his door.

He welcomed her with no surprise, no ceremony, and no desperation. Only with calm joy, like a host who had been expecting her all along.

She asked, "Aren't you shocked to see me?"

He replied, "Not shocked. I live each day in a way that honours your presence. You didn't come today – you were always here. You simply revealed yourself."

Lakshmi smiled. "Where I am honoured in spirit, I arrive in form."

Law of Attraction Insight:

Embody the energy first.
So many wait for the money to feel abundant.
Wait for love to feel worthy.
Wait for success to feel deserving.
But life mirrors your vibration, not your desire.
When you start dressing like, walking like, preparing like Lakshmi already lives in your space – she shows up.
Start now.
Make space.
Become the energy of what you wish to receive.

Theme: "Live like Lakshmi already lives in your home."

Daily Soul Practice

1. Write Your Most Burning Desire

But today, write it as if it's already yours.

My most burning desire is:

2. EFT Tapping Script (Repeat 3 Rounds)

Karate Chop Point:
"Even though I've felt lack before, I now choose to live as if it's already mine."

Eyebrow: I open my space to abundance

Side of Eye: I prepare for what I desire

Under Eye: I live like it's already done

Under Nose: Lakshmi already lives in my home

Chin: I treat myself like I am already rich

Collarbone: I prepare my world for blessings

Under Arm: I am worthy of receiving fully

Top of Head: I embody abundance now

Take 3 deep breaths. Drink water.

3. Letter to the Universe

Dear Universe,

Today, I stop waiting.

I begin becoming.

I align my energy, my space, and my thoughts with what I desire – because I know it's already on its way.

I walk with faith. I prepare with joy. I receive with grace.

Abundance is not a far-off dream – it's my current vibration.

Thank you for matching my energy with your miracles.

With joy,

With love,

(Your Name)

4. Intention Box Prompt

"I live as if Lakshmi already lives here. I embody the wealth I seek."

Write it. Feel it. Place it in your sacred space:

5. Journal Reflection

- **How am I preparing my space and energy for abundance?**
- **Where can I embody more of what I desire today?**
- **What does abundance feel like in my body?**

Reflection:

Day 4: Shaileya – Embody Abundance First

Theme: "Live like Lakshmi already lives in your home."

Energy Summary

Before: Waiting, hoping, feeling separate

After: Inviting, embodying, receiving

Shaileya didn't chase Lakshmi.

He created an inner and outer life that welcomed her.

Today, treat yourself like a divine guest is already home.

Because truly... she is.

Day 5: Ruchi – Visualisation is Construction

Theme: "My dream is already real within me."

Ruchi's Temple Vision

Rishi Ruchi was a devout sage known for his unshakable vision. He once decided to build a temple – not just of stone, but of spiritual perfection. But unlike others who began with land, labour, and donations, Ruchi began with his mind.

Each morning at dawn, he would enter deep meditation and see every detail:

The foundation is carved in sacred geometry.

The sanctum is glowing with divine light.

The sound of bells. The fragrance of flowers.

He visualised every corner – with love, clarity, and emotion.

Years passed, yet no stone was laid. People laughed, calling his "temple" imaginary.

But Ruchi smiled.

"A temple built in the field of consciousness," he said, "will soon demand form in the physical."

And it did.

One day, a group of travellers passing through had the same vivid dream – of a temple shining in the forest. They were led to Ruchi, and moved by his energy and clarity, they began building what he had already constructed in spirit.

Law of Attraction Insight:

See it. Feel it. It becomes real.
The world tells you to “be realistic.”
But manifestation begins in the unseen.
When you see it clearly and feel it deeply, your subconscious shifts.
When your energy shifts, so does your field.
And soon, reality bends to match what you've already lived within.
Don’t wait for proof.
Be the evidcnoo.

Daily Soul Practice

1. Write Your Most Burning Desire

Describe it in vivid detail – as if it already exists. Use all five senses.

My most burning desire is:

2. EFT Tapping Script (Repeat 3 Rounds)

Karate Chop Point:
"Even though I've doubted the power of my vision, I now believe it is already real."

Eyebrow: My vision is strong and sacred

Side of Eye: I see it clearly in my mind

Under Eye: I feel it in my body

Under Nose: My dream is already alive

Chin: My energy builds what my hands cannot

Collarbone: I trust the unseen to become seen

Under Arm: My vision is powerful

Top of Head: What I see is already coming to life

Take 3 deep breaths. Drink water.

Theme: "My dream is already real within me."

3. Letter to the Universe

Dear Universe,

Today, I choose to build from the inside out.

I hold my vision with clarity, love, and certainty – not because I see proof, but because I know energy precedes matter.

Every time I visualize, I am aligning with what is already mine.

Thank you for matching my inner reality with the perfect outer reflection.

With love,

(Your Name)

4. Intention Box Prompt

"My vision is real. My reality is catching up."

Write it down and place it with devotion:

Theme: "My dream is already real within me."

5. Journal Reflection

- **What does my dream life look, smell, sound, feel like?**
- **How can I bring elements of that vision into my space today?**
- **What proof do I already have that my dream is becoming real?**

Reflection:

Day 5: Ruchi – Visualisation is Construction

Theme: "My dream is already real within me."

Energy Summary

Before: Doubt, seeking validation, foggy vision

After: Clarity, deep belief, activated imagination

Like Ruchi, don't wait for others to believe.

Hold your vision sacred – and reality will follow.

Day 6: Maitreyi – Walk As the Final Self

Theme: "I already AM who I came to become."

Maitreyi – The Woman of Inner Wealth

In ancient India, Maitreyi was not just the wife of the great sage Yajnavalkya – she was a spiritual scholar in her own right, known for her fierce intellect and fearless questions about the meaning of life. When Yajnavalkya decided to renounce his worldly life, he offered to divide his material possessions between his two wives. Katayani accepted her share quietly. But Maitreyi asked:

"If all the wealth in the world were mine, would it make me immortal?"

Yajnavalkya replied, "No. Wealth cannot buy immortality."

Then Maitreyi, with unshaken presence, said:

"Then what shall I do with things that cannot make me eternal? Teach me what makes the soul immortal."

And so he did.

Maitreyi walked the rest of her life as the final self – not chasing identity, but embodying it.

She didn't wait for approval.

She didn't collect roles or titles.

She stood rooted in who she already was:

Divine. Complete. Unshakable.

Law of Attraction Insight:

Be her (or him or them). Now.

Most people wait to become –

To earn the title, to hit the number, to hear the applause.

But the Law of Attraction doesn't respond to delay.

It responds to identity.

The moment you start living as if it's already done,

The world shifts to reflect that reality.

When you walk as the final self, life follows your lead.

Theme: "I already AM who I came to become."

Daily Soul Practice

1. Write Your Most Burning Desire

Write it in present tense – like you're already living it. Speak from identity.

My most burning desire is:

2. EFT Tapping Script (Repeat 3 Rounds)

Karate Chop Point:

"Even though I sometimes forget who I am, I now choose to walk as my highest self."

Eyebrow: I already am her

Side of Eye: I walk with calm certainty

Under Eye: I release the need to prove

Under Nose: I embody my final self today

Chin: I let go of waiting

Collarbone: I show up in alignment

Under Arm: My energy is already home

Top of Head: I walk as the one I came here to be

Take 3 deep breaths. Drink water.

3. Letter to the Universse

Dear Universe,

Today, I stop seeking. I stop waiting.

I remember that I am already whole, already aligned, already divine.

Thank you for allowing me to walk as the one who already IS – not someday, not after I achieve more – but now

With love,
(Your Name)

4. Intention Box Prompt

"I already AM her/him/them. The rest is simply reflection."
Write it and drop it with belief:

5. Journal Reflection

- **Who is the version of me that already has it all?**
- **How can I act, speak, and move from that place today?**
- **What identity shift have I already embodied in the last 6 days?**

Reflection:

Day 6: Maitreyi – Walk As the Final Self

Theme: "I already AM who I came to become."

Energy Summary

Before: Seeking, waiting, over-efforting

After: Rootedness, presence, embodiment

Like Maitreyi, you don't have to collect more –

You just have to remember who you already are.

Day 7: Weekly Reflection – Witness Your Becoming

Theme: "I honor my journey and witness my growth."

The Journey of Becoming

In the ancient traditions, the path of the seeker is not measured by distant goals alone but by the awareness of each step taken. The journey itself holds the sacred alchemy of transformation.

The story of a great seeker reminds us that becoming is a process—a flow where every challenge, every small victory, and every moment of surrender shapes the evolving self. Just as rivers carve valleys over time, our inner landscape is molded by consistent presence and conscious reflection.

This story encourages us to pause and witness our becoming without judgment. To see how far we've come, to honour the lessons, and to prepare with gratitude for the unfolding path ahead.

Theme: "I honor my journey and witness my growth."

Law of Attraction Insight:

Reflection deepens your awareness and strengthens manifestation. By witnessing your growth, you align more deeply with your true self and your desires.

Reflection releases resistance, clarifies intentions, and energises your focus.

The universe responds to your conscious acknowledgment of progress.

Daily Soul Practice

1. Write Your Most Burning Desire

Revisit your desire with renewed clarity and gratitude.

My most burning desire is:

2. EFT Tapping Script (Repeat 3 Rounds)

Karate Chop Point:

"Even though sometimes I forget to honor my progress, I now choose to witness my becoming with love and gratitude."

Eyebrow: I honor my journey

Side of Eye: I see my growth clearly

Under Eye: I release self-judgment

Under Nose: I celebrate my efforts

Chin: I welcome lessons learned

Collarbone: I am proud of my progress

Under Arm: I trust the unfolding path

Top of Head: I witness my becoming

Take 3 deep breaths. Drink water.

3. Letter to the Universe

Dear Universe,
Today, I pause to honor my journey and growth.
Thank you for every step that shapes my becoming.
I trust the path unfolds perfectly in divine timing.

With love,
(Your Name)

4. Intention Box Prompt

"I witness my becoming with love and gratitude."

Write it and drop it with belief:

Theme: "I honor my journey and witness my growth."

5. Journal Reflection

- **What progress have I made this week?**
- **What lessons have helped me grow?**
- **How can I honor my journey and continue with trust?**

Reflection:

Day 7: Weekly Reflection – Witness Your Becoming

Theme: "I honor my journey and witness my growth."

Energy Summary

Before: Rushing, distracted, impatient

After: Grounded, aware, grateful

By witnessing your becoming, you strengthen your power to manifest rooted in presence and aligned with your true path.

Day 8: Arjuna's Eye – Pure Focus

Theme: "I keep my gaze unwavering on my goal."

Arjuna's Eye – The Warrior's Focus

In the great Indian epic Mahabharata, Arjuna was a peerless archer and warrior, famed for his precision and unwavering concentration. Before the battle of Kurukshetra, Arjuna was deeply troubled and confused about his duty and the morality of war. Seeking guidance, he turned to Lord Krishna, his charioteer and spiritual guide.

But long before that, as a young prince, Arjuna faced a test that would define his focus for life.

His guru, Dronacharya, wanted to teach him the value of single-minded concentration. One day, he asked Arjuna to aim his arrow at the eye of a spinning wooden bird perched high on a tree.

Dronacharya said:

"Look only at the bird's eye. Do not look at anything else. Do not let your mind wander."

Arjuna's eyes locked firmly on the tiny target. He ignored the tree, the branches, the movement of the leaves—his entire being was centered on the bird's eye. With a perfect shot, he pierced it exactly. That single moment of complete focus became his defining quality the power to see clearly through distractions and doubt, and to act decisively.

Years later, on the battlefield, this focus sustained him, allowing him to overcome internal struggles and fulfill his dharma as a warrior and seeker of truth.

He showed us that clarity of vision is the source of power.

Theme: "I keep my gaze unwavering on my goal."

Law of Attraction Insight:

Your energy flows where your attention goes.
When you focus with purity, the universe aligns effortlessly with your intent.
Distractions and doubts are illusions that dissipate when your gaze is steady.
Like Arjuna's arrow, your intentions hit the mark when your mind is still, clear, and unshakable.

Theme: "I keep my gaze unwavering on my goal."

Daily Soul Practice

1. Write Your Most Burning Desire

Focus only on the essence of what you want, as if already achieved.

My most burning desire is:

2. EFT Tapping Script (Repeat 3 Rounds)

Karate Chop Point:
"Even though distractions sometimes pull me away, I now choose to keep my focus pure and steady."

Eyebrow: I lock my gaze on my goal

Side of Eye: My mind is clear and calm

Under Eye: I release all doubts and distractions

Under Nose: I am fully present in this moment

Chin: I act with purpose and clarity

Collarbone: My focus sharpens with each breath

Under Arm: I trust the path unfolding before me

Top of Head: I shoot my arrow straight to my target

Take 3 deep breaths. Drink water.

3. Letter to the Universe

Dear Universe,

Today, I vow to keep my vision clear and unwavering.

I release all distractions and doubts that cloud my mind.

Thank you for aligning my path with my highest focus and true intention.

With steadfast heart and sharp eyes,

(Your Name)

4. Intention Box Prompt

"My focus is pure. My aim is true. I hit my target with clarity and grace."

Write it and drop it with belief:

5. Journal Reflection

- **What distractions have pulled me away in the past, and how can I gently bring my focus back?**
- **How does it feel to have perfect clarity in my mind and heart?**
- **What would I accomplish if I maintained unwavering focus all day?**

Reflection:

Day 8: Arjuna's Eye – Pure Focus

Theme: "I keep my gaze unwavering on my goal."

Energy Summary

Before: Scattered, overwhelmed, unfocused

After: Clear, centered, powerful

Like Arjuna, your strength lies in your focused eye – the power to see your true path and follow it with unwavering precision.

Day 9: Ekalavya's Practice – Inner Devotion Magnetizes Results

Theme: "My dedication draws my desires to me effortlessly."

The Power of Devotion and Discipline

In the epic Mahabharata, Ekalavya was a young tribal prince who dreamed of becoming a master archer. He sought to learn from the great teacher Dronacharya but was rejected because he did not belong to the royal class.

Undeterred, Ekalavya fashioned a clay statue of Dronacharya and practiced diligently before it every day, treating the statue as his true guru.

Through unwavering devotion, relentless practice, and absolute faith, Ekalavya mastered archery beyond expectation – becoming one of the finest archers in the land.

When Dronacharya discovered this, he asked Ekalavya for his right thumb as guru dakshina (teacher's fee), knowing it would limit his ability but honouring the sacred tradition. Without hesitation, Ekalavya gave it, demonstrating humility and respect.

Ekalavya's story teaches us that true mastery arises from inner devotion and self-discipline – even without external validation or resources.

Theme: "My dedication draws my desires to me effortlessly."

Law of Attraction Insight:

Your inner devotion is a powerful magnet that pulls results toward you.
When your heart is fully committed and your practice consistent, the universe responds with abundance.
Effort mixed with love and faith creates an unstoppable force that moves mountains.
Results flow naturally when you honour your inner guru and keep showing up.

Daily Soul Practice

1. Write Your Most Burning Desire

Declare your desire with the dedication of a devoted student.

My most burning desire is:

2. EFT Tapping Script (Repeat 3 Rounds)

Karate Chop Point:
"Even though I sometimes doubt my progress, I now choose to trust my inner devotion to guide me."

Eyebrow: I commit to my practice

Side of Eye: My heart is fully devoted

Under Eye: I release all impatience

Under Nose: I honor my inner teacher

Chin: I show up with discipline and faith

Collarbone: Results flow to me effortlessly

Under Arm: My dedication is magnetic

Top of Head: I am a magnet for success

Take 3 deep breaths. Drink water.

3. Letter to the Universe

Dear Universe,

Today, I dedicate myself fully to my practice and purpose.

I trust that my inner devotion draws all that I need to me effortlessly.

Thank you for honoring my commitment with abundant results.

With unwavering faith,

(Your Name)

4. Intention Box Prompt

"My devotion is my power. My practice creates my reality."
Write it and drop it with belief:

5. Journal Reflection

- **How can I deepen my devotion to my goal today?**
- **What small daily discipline can I commit to without fail?**
- **How does consistent practice shift my mindset and results?**

Reflection:

Day 9: Ekalavya's Practice – Inner Devotion Magnetizes Results

Theme: "My dedication draws my desires to me effortlessly."

Energy Summary

Before: Doubtful, inconsistent, searching

After: Devoted, disciplined, magnetised

Like Ekalavya, your true strength lies in your inner devotion – the steady flame that magnetises your dreams into reality.

Day 10: Markandeya & Shiva – Faith Overrides Timelines

Theme: "My faith is stronger than time and circumstance."

Markandeya – The Boy Who Defied Death

Markandeya was a devoted young boy destined to die at the age of 16, as foretold by the god of death, Yama. From birth, he was deeply immersed in devotion to Lord Shiva, spending his days chanting prayers and meditating with unwavering faith.

As his destined time approached, Yama came to claim his soul. But Markandeya clung to a Shiva Lingam statue, seeking the Lord's protection with absolute trust.

Moved by his devotion and courage, Lord Shiva appeared in a blaze of divine light, intervening to protect the boy. He defeated Yama and granted Markandeya immortality, blessing him with eternal life as a symbol of faith's power to transcend fate and time.

Markandeya's story teaches us that faith is not bound by timelines or conditions – it has the power to rewrite destiny itself

Theme: "My faith is stronger than time and circumstance."

Law of Attraction Insight:

Faith acts as the ultimate catalyst in manifesting your desires. When you trust fully, even without visible proof or immediate results, you align yourself with the infinite flow of the universe.

Time becomes a servant to your faith, not a master.

The moment you release resistance and surrender to belief, the impossible becomes possible.

Daily Soul Practice

1. Write Your Most Burning Desire

Declare your desire with unshakeable faith in its manifestation.

My most burning desire is:

2. EFT Tapping Script (Repeat 3 Rounds)

Karate Chop Point:
"Even though I sometimes doubt the timing of my dreams, I now choose to trust in the divine timing of the universe."

Eyebrow: I have faith beyond all limits

Side of Eye: I surrender to divine timing

Under Eye: I release all impatience

Under Nose: I trust the path unfolding for me

Chin: I believe my desires are already mine

Collarbone: Time works in my favour

Under Arm: I am patient and persistent

Top of Head: My faith overrides all timelines

Take 3 deep breaths. Drink water.

3. Letter to the Universe

Dear Universe,

Today, I surrender all doubts about when and how.

I trust that everything is aligning perfectly in divine timing.

Thank you for supporting me with faith that moves mountains.

With deep trust and surrender,

(Your Name)

4. Intention Box Prompt

"My faith is unshakeable. Timing is perfect. I receive all in divine order."

Write it and drop it with belief:

5. Journal Reflection

- **Where do I feel resistance around timing or outcomes?**
- **How can I cultivate deeper faith and patience today?**
- **What signs of divine timing have I noticed in my journey?**

Reflection:

Day 10: Markandeya & Shiva – Faith Overrides Timelines

Theme: "My faith is stronger than time and circumstance."

Energy Summary

Before: Doubtful, anxious, rushing

After: Faithful, patient, surrendered

Like Markandeya, your faith holds the power to override any timeline transforming your journey with divine grace and eternal trust.

Day 11: Sudama & Krishna – Humble Giving Brings Returns

Theme: "I give with humility and receive with grace."

Sudama – The Power of Humble Giving

Sudama was a poor but devoted childhood friend of Lord Krishna. Though he lived in poverty, his heart was rich with love and humility. When life's hardships weighed heavily on Sudama, he decided to visit Krishna's palace to seek help. Though he carried a simple gift of beaten rice, he felt ashamed of his poverty and modest offering. Krishna welcomed him with open arms, honoring their friendship without judgment or pride. He accepted Sudama's humble gift with deep love and gratitude.

Without Sudama realising it, Krishna blessed him abundantly. When Sudama returned home, he found his humble hut transformed into a palace filled with wealth and happiness.

This story reminds us that the energy of giving—no matter how small or simple—is powerful and always returns multiplied when offered with a pure heart.

Theme: "I give with humility and receive with grace."

Law of Attraction Insight:

Giving with humility opens the channels of abundance.
The universe reciprocates generosity that flows from genuine kindness without expectation.
When you release pride and offer freely, you magnetise blessings beyond measure.
True wealth comes from the joy of giving, not just receiving.

Daily Soul Practice

1. Write Your Most Burning Desire

Express your desire with an open and generous heart.

My most burning desire is:

2. EFT Tapping Script (Repeat 3 Rounds)

Karate Chop Point:
"Even though I sometimes hold back from giving fully, I now choose to give humbly and receive graciously."

Eyebrow: I give with an open heart

Side of Eye: My gifts flow freely

Under Eye: I release all fears of lack

Under Nose: I welcome abundance in return

Chin: I am grateful for all I receive

Collarbone: Giving brings me joy

Under Arm: I trust the flow of generosity

Top of Head: I am a channel for abundance

Take 3 deep breaths. Drink water.

3. Letter to the Universe

Dear Universe,

Today, I offer my gifts with humility and love.

I trust that my giving returns to me multiplied in many forms.

Thank you for the endless flow of abundance through me.

With a grateful heart,

(Your Name)

4. Intention Box Prompt

"I give freely and humbly. I receive blessings with gratitude."

Write it and drop it with belief:

5. Journal Reflection

- **How can I give more freely without attachment or expectation?**
- **What blessings have come to me through acts of humble giving?**
- **How does generosity transform my sense of abundance?**

Reflection:

Day 11: Sudama & Krishna – Humble Giving Brings Returns

Theme: "I give with humility and receive with grace."

Energy Summary

Before: Hesitant, guarded, scarce

After: Open, generous, abundant

Like Sudama, your humble giving creates a powerful ripple – bringing blessings back to you in unexpected and beautiful ways.

Day 12: Nachiketa & Yama – Ask Beyond What's Visible

Theme: "I seek the truth beyond appearances."

Nachiketa – The Seeker Who Questioned Death

Nachiketa was a young boy known for his courage and curiosity. When his father offered him to the god of death, Yama, as a token of a ritual, Nachiketa did not fear. Instead, he waited patiently for Yama's arrival.

When Yama appeared, Nachiketa respectfully asked three profound questions—about life, death, and what lies beyond the physical world.

Yama tried to distract him with worldly pleasures and promises but Nachiketa remained steadfast, asking for the ultimate truth: what happens after death?

Impressed by his determination and sincerity, Yama revealed the secrets of the soul's immortality, the nature of the self, and the path to liberation.

Nachiketa's story teaches us to look beyond the surface and ask the deeper questions that reveal our true essence.

Theme: "I seek the truth beyond appearances."

Law of Attraction Insight:

True manifestation requires seeking beyond the obvious.
When you ask beyond what's visible, you tap into deeper wisdom and alignment.
Questions fuel clarity and open doors unseen to the casual observer.
Your growth and results expand as you explore beyond surface appearances.

Daily Soul Practice

1. Write Your Most Burning Desire

Ask your heart not only what you want, but why and how at a deeper level.

My most burning desire is:

2. EFT Tapping Script (Repeat 3 Rounds)

Karate Chop Point:

"Even though I sometimes accept surface answers, I now choose to seek the deeper truth within."

Eyebrow: I question what lies beneath

Side of Eye: I release all doubts and distractions

Under Eye: I open to hidden wisdom

Under Nose: I ask beyond appearances

Chin: I seek the truth fearlessly

Collarbone: I align with my highest knowing

Under Arm: I trust the unseen path

Top of Head: I am open to deeper guidance

Take 3 deep breaths. Drink water.

3. Letter to the Universe

Dear Universe,

Today, I vow to ask beyond what is visible and seek deeper truths.

Thank you for guiding me to clarity, wisdom, and alignment.

With open heart and mind,

(Your Name)

4. Intention Box Prompt

"I seek truth beyond appearances. I trust what lies beneath."
Write it and drop it with belief:

5. Journal Reflection

- **What surface answers am I ready to question?**
- **Where can I explore deeper wisdom in my life and goals?**
- **How can seeking beyond appearances transform my journey?**

Reflection:

Day 12: Nachiketa & Yama – Ask Beyond What's Visible

Theme: "I seek the truth beyond appearances."

Energy Summary

Before: Accepting, unclear, surface-level

After: Curious, aligned, deeply aware

Like Nachiketa, your fearless questions lead you beyond illusions – toward truth, clarity, and profound manifestation.

Day 13: King Janaka – Stillness and Success Coexist

Theme: "I embody calm presence while achieving my highest goals."

King Janaka – The Wise King Who Ruled with Stillness

King Janaka was known as a great ruler, philosopher, and spiritual seeker. Despite his immense responsibilities, wealth, and power, he was deeply peaceful and unattached.
Janaka exemplified the rare balance of worldly success and inner stillness. While managing his kingdom wisely and effectively, he maintained a calm mind, free from anxiety and distraction.
When sages came to test his wisdom, Janaka showed that true mastery comes not just from action, but from a centred and still mind – a presence that remains unshaken regardless of outer circumstances.
His life teaches us that success is not about frantic effort but about embodying stillness amid activity.

Law of Attraction Insight:

Stillness is the fertile ground where your desires grow.
When your mind is calm, you create space for inspiration, clarity, and aligned action.
Success follows naturally when you are present and centred, not when you chase or force outcomes.
The universe meets you in your stillness and mirrors your calm strength.

Daily Soul Practice

1. Write Your Most Burning Desire

Write your desire from a place of peaceful presence and certainty.
My most burning desire is:

2. EFT Tapping Script (Repeat 3 Rounds)

Karate Chop Point:
"Even though I sometimes feel rushed or anxious, I now choose to embody stillness and calm success."

Eyebrow: I am calm and centered

Side of Eye: My mind is peaceful and clear

Under Eye: I release all tension and worry

Under Nose: I trust in divine timing

Chin: I act with calm confidence

Collarbone: Stillness brings me success

Under Arm: I am present in every moment

Top of Head: I embody calm and power

Take 3 deep breaths. Drink water.

Theme: "I embody calm presence while achieving my highest goals."

3. Letter to the Universe

Dear Universe,

Today, I embody stillness and trust in my journey.

I know that calm presence and success coexist within me.

Thank you for guiding me with peace and clarity.

With serene confidence,

(Your Name)

4. Intention Box Prompt

"I am still. I am successful. I trust my path unfolds with grace."
Write it and drop it with belief:

5. Journal Reflection

- **Where in my life can I cultivate more stillness?**
- **How does calm presence influence my actions and results?**
- **What successes have come when I trusted and stayed centered?**

Reflection:

Day 13: King Janaka – Stillness and Success Coexist

Theme: "I embody calm presence while achieving my highest goals."

Energy Summary

Before: Anxious, hurried, scattered

After: Calm, centred, empowered

Like King Janaka, your success flows from a still mind –
a peaceful presence that creates powerful results effortlessly.

Day 14: Shabari & Rama – Divine Timing Responds to Readiness

Theme: "I trust that the right moment arrives when I am ready."

Shabari – The Devoted Seeker and Divine Patience

Shabari was a humble woman known for her unwavering devotion and patience. She spent years waiting for Lord Rama's visit, preparing her heart and home to receive him.

Though she belonged to a marginalised tribe, her love and sincerity were pure. Every day, she carefully tasted the berries she offered Rama to ensure they were sweet and perfect – a symbol of her devotion and readiness.

When Lord Rama finally arrived, he accepted her offering with deep gratitude and respect, recognising her pure heart beyond all social boundaries.

Shabari's story teaches us that divine timing unfolds perfectly when we are ready inside. Patience and readiness magnetise grace and blessings.

Law of Attraction Insight:

The universe moves in harmony with your inner readiness.
When you prepare your mind, heart, and spirit, the right opportunities flow effortlessly to you.
Patience is not waiting passively but cultivating readiness to receive.
Trust that your desires come at the perfect moment aligned with your highest good.

Daily Soul Practice

1. Write Your Most Burning Desire

Declare your desire with trust in divine timing and your readiness.

My most burning desire is:

2. EFT Tapping Script (Repeat 3 Rounds)

Karate Chop Point:
"Even though I sometimes feel impatient, I now choose to trust divine timing and prepare myself fully."

Eyebrow: I am ready to receive

Side of Eye: I trust perfect timing

Under Eye: I release all impatience

Under Nose: I cultivate patience and faith

Chin: I prepare my heart and mind

Collarbone: Blessings come at the right time

Under Arm: I am aligned with my highest good

Top of Head: Divine timing unfolds for me

Take 3 deep breaths. Drink water.

3. Letter to the Universe

Dear Universe,
Today, I trust that everything arrives when I am ready.
I prepare my heart and mind to receive with gratitude and grace.
hank you for guiding me with perfect divine timing.

With faith and patience,
(Your Name)

4. Intention Box Prompt

"I trust divine timing. I am ready to receive all blessings."
Write it and drop it with belief:

5. Journal Reflection

- **Where can I cultivate more patience and readiness in my life?**
- **How does trusting divine timing ease my journey?**
- **What signs of divine timing have I witnessed recently?**

Reflection:

Day 14: Shabari & Rama – Divine Timing Responds to Readiness

Theme: "I trust that the right moment arrives when I am ready."

Energy Summary

Before: Impatient, restless, uncertain

After: Patient, prepared, trusting

Like Shabari, your devotion and readiness invite divine grace – bringing blessings in perfect timing to your life.

Day 15: Samudra Manthan – Nectar Comes After Resistance

Theme: "I embrace challenges as the gateway to my sweetest success."

Samudra Manthan – The Churning of the Ocean of Milk

In ancient Indian mythology, the gods (Devas) and demons (Asuras) came together to churn the vast Ocean of Milk to obtain Amrita – the nectar of immortality.

Using Mount Mandara as the churning rod and the serpent Vasuki as the rope, they pulled tirelessly back and forth, facing immense resistance and obstacles.

The ocean churned fiercely, releasing many things—both poisonous and precious. The gods used divine intervention to neutralise the poison and finally secured the nectar, symbolising ultimate bliss and immortality.

This epic tale teaches us that true rewards and transformation emerge only after enduring resistance and upheaval. The sweetest success follows persistent effort through challenges.

Theme: "I embrace challenges as the gateway to my sweetest success."

Law of Attraction Insight:

Resistance is a sign that your manifestation is near.
The universe tests your commitment through challenges, refining your focus and strength.
When you embrace obstacles as part of your journey, you open yourself to greater abundance and growth.
Persistence through difficulty turns turmoil into your nectar of success.

Daily Soul Practice

1. Write Your Most Burning Desire

Declare your desire with courage and readiness to face challenges.
My most burning desire is:

2. EFT Tapping Script (Repeat 3 Rounds)

Karate Chop Point:
"Even though resistance sometimes discourages me, I now choose to embrace challenges as steps toward my success."

Eyebrow: I welcome challenges

Side of Eye: Resistance makes me stronger

Under Eye: I release fear of struggle

Under Nose: I trust the process fully

Chin: I persist with courage and faith

Collarbone: Every challenge brings me closer

Under Arm: I am patient through difficulty

Top of Head: Nectar comes after resistance

Take 3 deep breaths. Drink water.

Theme: "I embrace challenges as the gateway to my sweetest success."

3. Letter to the Universe

Dear Universe,

Today, I welcome resistance as a sign of growth.

I trust that my perseverance will bring sweet rewards.

Thank you for strengthening me through every challenge.

With courage and faith,

(Your Name)

4. Intention Box Prompt

"I embrace challenges. I receive my sweetest success."

Write it and drop it with belief:

5. Journal Reflection

- **What challenges am I currently facing, and how can I shift my perspective to see them as growth?**
- **How has overcoming past resistance led to success in my life?**
- **What strengths have I gained through difficulties?**

Reflection:

Day 15: Samudra Manthan – Nectar Comes After Resistance

Theme: “I embrace challenges as the gateway to my sweetest success.”

Energy Summary

Before: Frustrated, discouraged, resistant

After: Empowered, patient, resilient

Like the Samudra Manthan, your greatest nectar awaits beyond the struggle – offering transformation and lasting success through your steadfastness.

Day 16: Draupadi's Surrender – Surrender is Real Power

Theme: "I release control and trust in the greater flow."

Draupadi – The Strength in Surrender

Draupadi, the queen of the Pandavas in the Mahabharata, was renowned not only for her beauty but for her strength, wisdom, and dignity. Throughout her life, she faced unimaginable hardships—betrayal, humiliation, and challenges that tested her spirit beyond limits.

One of the most powerful moments in her story is during the infamous dice game in the Kaurava court. Her husbands, the Pandavas, lost everything in the game, including Draupadi herself. She was dragged into the assembly, humiliated publicly as Duryodhana and his brothers sought to dishonour her.

Despite the overwhelming injustice, Draupadi did not fall into despair or anger. Instead, in that critical moment, she turned inward and surrendered completely to Lord Krishna, the divine protector. She trusted in his divine power to shield her from harm, even as the odds were stacked against her.

Miraculously, as the cruel attempt was made to disrobe her, Krishna's divine grace enveloped Draupadi, protecting her modesty by endlessly extending her sari, so no harm could come. Her surrender was not passive submission but an active, courageous trust in the cosmic order beyond the apparent chaos.

This surrender preserved her dignity and power, showing that true strength lies in yielding to divine will rather than struggling in ego-driven resistance. Draupadi's story teaches us that surrendering control does not mean giving up – it means opening ourselves to the infinite support and wisdom of the universe.

Law of Attraction Insight:

True power arises when you surrender resistance.
Releasing the need to control outcomes opens space for miracles and flow.
When you trust fully, you align with the infinite intelligence of the universe.
Surrender invites divine support and effortless manifestation.

Daily Soul Practice

1. Write Your Most Burning Desire

Write your desire with trust and openness to the highest good.

My most burning desire is:

2. EFT Tapping Script (Repeat 3 Rounds)

Karate Chop Point:
"Even though I sometimes struggle to let go, I now choose to surrender and trust the universe."

Eyebrow: I release control

Side of Eye: I trust divine timing

Under Eye: I let go of resistance

Under Nose: I open to miracles

Chin: I surrender with courage

Collarbone: I welcome divine support

Under Arm: I flow with the universe

Top of Head: Surrender is my true power

Take 3 deep breaths. Drink water.

3. Letter to the Universe

Dear Universe,

Today, I surrender my need to control outcomes.

I trust that your wisdom guides me perfectly.

Thank you for supporting me with infinite love and grace.

With open heart and faith,

[Your Name]

4. Intention Box Prompt

"I surrender and trust. I am supported always."

Write it and drop it with belief:

5. Journal Reflection

- **Where am I holding onto control too tightly?**
- **How can surrender open new pathways in my life?**
- **What support can I welcome by letting go?**

Reflection:

Day 16: Draupadi's Surrender – Surrender is Real Power

Theme: "I release control and trust in the greater flow."

Energy Summary

Before: Struggling, resisting, anxious

After: Trusting, flowing, empowered

Like Draupadi, your surrender is your real power –

a gateway to grace, miracles, and effortless success.

Day 17: Sage Vishwamitra – From Chaos to Mastery

Theme: "I transform inner chaos into clear mastery."

Vishwamitra – The Journey from Tempest to Triumph

Vishwamitra was once a powerful king named Kaushika, known for his strength and ambition but also for his temper and restlessness. Despite his worldly power, he felt a deep yearning for spiritual wisdom and mastery over his mind and the universe.

His journey to become one of the greatest sages began with intense struggle. In the early days, Vishwamitra's mind was like a raging storm – full of pride, anger, and confusion. He faced many internal battles as well as external opposition from gods, sages, and demons.

Determined to transcend his human limitations, Vishwamitra undertook severe austerities and relentless meditation. He faced temptations, doubts, and fierce trials that challenged his resolve. At one point, his anger flared so intensely that it threatened to consume him and those around him.

But through unwavering discipline, self-reflection, and surrender, Vishwamitra gradually tamed the chaos within. He learned to channel his energy with precision, turning wild emotions into focused power.

His transformation culminated when he received the title "Vishwamitra" – meaning "Friend of the Universe" – a master who balanced strength with wisdom, chaos with calm. His story shows us that mastery is born not from ease but through embracing and transforming our inner storms.

Law of Attraction Insight:

Chaos within signals growth and transformation ahead.
When you face your inner turmoil with courage, you clear the path for mastery and manifestation.
Disorder and resistance are the raw materials for your focused power.
By embracing and directing your energy, you create clarity and attract your highest potential.

Daily Soul Practice

1. Write Your Most Burning Desire

Declare your desire with clarity born from inner mastery.

My most burning desire is:

2. EFT Tapping Script (Repeat 3 Rounds)

Karate Chop Point:

"Even though my mind sometimes feels chaotic, I now choose to transform this energy into focused mastery."

Eyebrow: I embrace my inner storm

Side of Eye: I release confusion and doubt

Under Eye: I channel my energy with clarity

Under Nose: I am calm amidst chaos

Chin: I transform challenges into power

Collarbone: I master my thoughts and emotions

Under Arm: I attract clarity and success

Top of Head: I am a friend of the universe

Take 3 deep breaths. Drink water.

3. Letter to the Universe

Dear Universe,

Today, I embrace my inner chaos as a path to mastery.
I trust that every challenge brings me closer to my highest self.
Thank you for guiding me from confusion to clarity.

With focused heart and mind,
(Your Name)

4. Intention Box Prompt

"I transform chaos into mastery. I attract clarity and power."

Write it and drop it with belief:

5. Journal Reflection

- **What areas of my life feel chaotic right now?**
- **How can I channel this energy toward mastery?**
- **What past experiences show my ability to transform challenges?**

Reflection:

Day 17: Sage Vishwamitra – From Chaos to Mastery

Theme: “I transform inner chaos into clear mastery.”

Energy Summary

Before: Confused, scattered, overwhelmed

After: Focused, calm, empowered

Like Sage Vishwamitra, your journey from chaos to mastery reveals your true power as a creator and a friend of the universe.

Day 18: King Harishchandra – Truth is a Vibration

Theme: "I align my life with the vibration of truth."

King Harishchandra – The King Who Lived Truth

King Harishchandra was renowned for his unwavering commitment to truth and integrity. His story is one of the most powerful examples of living in alignment with the highest principle—truth—no matter the cost.

Harishchandra was tested by the gods themselves, who challenged his resolve by stripping him of his kingdom, wealth, and even separating him from his family. Yet, through every hardship, he refused to waver from his promise to always speak and live the truth.

He worked as a humble servant, endured intense suffering, and faced grave trials without abandoning his integrity. His dedication was so pure and his vibration so strong that, in the end, the gods restored his kingdom and reunited him with his family, honouring his supreme devotion to truth.

Harishchandra's story teaches us that truth is more than words—it is a powerful vibration that shapes our reality. When you embody truth, you create harmony, trust, and alignment in your life and attract the highest good.

Law of Attraction Insight:

Truth is a vibration that resonates through all aspects of life.
When you live authentically and align with your inner truth, you magnetize genuine abundance and peace.
Falsehood and denial create resistance and block manifestation.
Honouring truth opens the flow of trust, clarity, and effortless success.

Daily Soul Practice

1. Write Your Most Burning Desire

Declare your desire with honesty and authenticity.
My most burning desire is:

2. EFT Tapping Script (Repeat 3 Rounds)

Karate Chop Point:
"Even though I sometimes struggle to be fully truthful, I now choose to align with my highest truth."

Eyebrow: I honor my authentic self

Side of Eye: I speak my truth with courage

Under Eye: I release fear of judgment

Under Nose: I embody honesty in all I do

Chin: I live in alignment with truth

Collarbone: Truth flows through me like light

Under Arm: I attract trust and clarity

Top of Head: I am vibration of truth

Take 3 deep breaths. Drink water.

3. Letter to the Universse

Dear Universe,
Today, I commit to living and speaking my truth fully.
I trust that my authenticity brings harmony and abundance.
Thank you for guiding me on the path of honesty and clarity.

With integrity and courage,
[Your Name]

4. Intention Box Prompt

"I am truth in vibration. I attract clarity and trust."
Write it and drop it with belief:

5. Journal Reflection

- **Where can I be more honest with myself and others?**
- **How does living my truth affect my energy and relationships?**
- **What blocks dissolve when I choose authenticity?**

Reflection:

Day 18: King Harishchandra – Truth is a Vibration

Theme: "I align my life with the vibration of truth."

Energy Summary

Before: Conflicted, guarded, uncertain

After: Authentic, clear, magnetic

Like King Harishchandra, your commitment to truth vibrates through your life – creating alignment, trust, and effortless flow.

Day 19: Sage Vashishta vs. Vishwamitra – Grace Over Ego

Theme: "I choose grace over ego in every moment."

The Tale of Sage Vashishta and Vishwamitra – Mastery Through Humility

Sage Vashishta was a revered rishi known for his deep wisdom, calm presence, and immense spiritual power. Vishwamitra, once a powerful king turned aspiring sage, was determined to match and surpass Vashishta's mastery.

Their story is filled with moments of rivalry, challenge, and intense spiritual tests. Vishwamitra's pride and ego often fueled his efforts, driving him to undertake severe austerities and powerful tapasya (meditation). Yet, despite his great power, his ego became a barrier to true mastery.

Vashishta, on the other hand, embodied grace—an effortless flow that comes from humility and surrender to the divine will. He remained grounded, teaching that spiritual power is not about proving oneself but about embodying compassion, patience, and inner peace.

In many instances, Vishwamitra's ego led to failures or conflicts, while Vashishta's grace attracted divine support and profound insight. Over time, Vishwamitra learned that surrendering ego opened the path to true wisdom and peace.

This story teaches us that grace, not ego, is the key to lasting mastery and fulfilment. When we release pride and embrace humility, we align with a higher power that guides and supports us effortlessly.

Law of Attraction Insight:

Ego creates resistance; grace creates flow.
When you release the need to prove and control, you open to divine support.
Grace attracts opportunities, wisdom, and ease.
Humility softens the heart and expands your capacity to receive.

Theme: "I choose grace over ego in every moment."

Daily Soul Practice

1. Write Your Most Burning Desire

Write your desire with a humble and open heart.

My most burning desire is:

2. EFT Tapping Script (Repeat 3 Rounds)

Karate Chop Point:
"Even though I sometimes let ego get in the way, I now choose to embrace grace and humility."

Eyebrow: I release pride and resistance

Side of Eye: I open to divine guidance

Under Eye: I choose humility over ego

Under Nose: I flow with grace and ease

Chin: I surrender the need to prove

Collarbone: Grace leads me to mastery

Under Arm: I accept support with gratitude

Top of Head: I embody grace over ego

Take 3 deep breaths. Drink water.

3. Letter to the Universe

Dear Universe,
Today, I release ego and choose grace in all I do.
I trust that humility opens the door to true mastery and peace.
Thank you for guiding me with compassion and light.

With an open and humble heart,
(Your Name)

....
....
....
....
....
....
....
....
....
....
....
....
....
....
....

4. Intention Box Prompt

"I choose grace over ego. I flow with divine support."

Write it and drop it with belief:

5. Journal Reflection

- **Where is ego blocking my growth and flow?**
- **How can I practice more humility and grace today?**
- **What support do I receive when I surrender pride?**

Reflection:

Day 19: Sage Vashishta vs. Vishwamitra – Grace Over Ego

Theme: "I choose grace over ego in every moment."

Energy Summary

Before: Defensive, prideful, resistant

After: Open, humble, flowing

Like Sage Vashishta, your grace dissolves ego – opening the path to mastery, peace, and divine alignment.

Day 20: Bhagiratha Brings Ganga – Desire Moves the Universe

Theme: "I move the universe with the power of my pure desire."

Bhagiratha – The King Who Moved Heaven and Earth

King Bhagiratha was a devoted and determined ruler whose ancestors' souls were trapped in hell, unable to find peace. To liberate them, Bhagiratha set out on a seemingly impossible mission: to bring the sacred river Ganga down from the heavens to Earth.

This task was monumental. The mighty Ganga flowed in the heavens with tremendous force, and bringing her to Earth risked destruction. Bhagiratha's intense penance and unwavering desire moved the hearts of gods and sages alike.

He performed severe austerities for thousands of years, his burning desire illuminating the cosmos. Finally, Lord Shiva agreed to help. He caught the raging river in his matted hair, controlling its powerful descent to the Earth, thus saving the world from devastation.

Bhagiratha's story reveals that pure, focused desire has the power to move even the most formidable forces of nature and the universe. When your intent is strong and aligned, the cosmos conspires to support you.

Theme: "I move the universe with the power of my pure desire."

Law of Attraction Insight:

Desire is the energy that initiates creation and movement.
When you hold a pure, unwavering desire, you send ripples through the universe.
Persistence and alignment amplify your ability to manifest miracles.
The universe responds to the clarity and intensity of your heart's true wish.

Theme: "I move the universe with the power of my pure desire."

Daily Soul Practice

1. Write Your Most Burning Desire

Declare your desire with pure, focused intention.
My most burning desire is:

2. EFT Tapping Script (Repeat 3 Rounds)

Karate Chop Point:

"Even though sometimes my desire feels distant, I now choose to focus and move the universe with my intention."

Eyebrow: My desire is pure and strong

Side of Eye: I release doubt and hesitation

Under Eye: I focus with unwavering faith

Under Nose: I trust the universe supports me

Chin: I persist with passion and clarity

Collarbone: My desire moves mountains

Under Arm: I am aligned with my highest good

Top of Head: I move the universe with my heart

Take 3 deep breaths. Drink water.

3. Letter to the Universe

Dear Universe,
Today, I ignite my desire with clarity and passion.
I trust that my pure intention moves mountains and opens doors.
Thank you for supporting me with cosmic strength.

With determined heart,
(Your Name)

....
....
....
....
....
....
....
....
....
....
....
....
....
....
....

4. Intention Box Prompt

"My desire is pure, strong, and unstoppable. The universe moves with me."

Write it and drop it with belief:

....

....

....

....

....

....

....

....

....

....

....

....

....

....

....

5. Journal Reflection

- **How clear and focused is my current desire?**
- **Where can I amplify my faith and persistence?**
- **What signs show that the universe is moving in my favor?**

Reflection:

Day 20: Bhagiratha Brings Ganga – Desire Moves the Universe

Theme: "I move the universe with the power of my pure desire."

Energy Summary

Before: Scattered, unsure, hesitant

After: Focused, determined, empowered

Like King Bhagiratha, your pure desire has the power to move the universe and manifest the impossible.

Day 21: Completion – The Identity is the Manifestation

Theme: "I embody my fulfilled desire as my true identity."

The Principle of Completion and Manifestation

In the ancient teachings, it is said that manifestation is not merely about acquiring something new outside but about fully becoming the energy and identity of what you desire.

The universe responds most powerfully when your inner identity matches your outer desires. When the sage or seeker completes their inner transformation—shedding doubt, fear, and resistance—they naturally step into the reality they have long sought.

This principle is echoed in many Vedic stories, where heroes and sages do not just reach their goals but become the embodiment of their aspirations. Their identity shifts first, and the external world follows suit, reflecting the inner truth.

Completion is the moment where desire dissolves into fulfillment, and the seeker knows: "I am already that which I wished to become." This alignment between identity and manifestation is the ultimate key to lasting success and joy.

Day 21: Completion – The Identity is the Manifestation

Theme: "I embody my fulfilled desire as my true identity."

Law of Attraction Insight:

Your identity creates your reality.

When you live, think, and feel as the person who already has what you desire, you magnetise your manifestation effortlessly.

Completion is the full embrace of your fulfilled self—no longer waiting or striving.

By embodying your desires now, you invite the universe to reflect that truth to you.

Daily Soul Practice

1. Write Your Most Burning Desire

Write your desire as if it is fully realized and part of who you are.

My most burning desire is:

2. EFT Tapping Script (Repeat 3 Rounds)

Karate Chop Point:

"Even though sometimes I doubt my fulfillment, I now choose to embody my desire as my true identity."

Eyebrow: I am already complete

Side of Eye: I live as my fulfilled self

Under Eye: I release all doubt and waiting

Under Nose: I embody my highest reality

Chin: I claim my manifestation now

Collarbone: I am whole and abundant

Under Arm: I walk in alignment with my desires

Top of Head: My identity is my manifestation

Take 3 deep breaths. Drink water.

3. Letter to the Universse

Dear Universe,

Dear Universe,

Today, I declare that I am already my fulfilled desire.

I step into this identity with full trust and joy.

Thank you for reflecting my true self in my reality.

With gratitude and certainty,

(Your Name)

4. Intention Box Prompt

"My identity is my manifestation. I am complete now."

Write it and drop it with belief:

5. Journal Reflection

- **How can I embody my fulfilled desire in thoughts, feelings, and actions today?**
- **What identity shifts have helped me manifest in the past?**
- **Where do I still hold resistance to completion?**

Reflection:

Day 21: Completion – The Identity is the Manifestation

Theme: "I embody my fulfilled desire as my true identity."

Energy Summary

Before: Waiting, doubting, striving

After: Embodying, aligned, fulfilled

Completion is the sacred union where identity and manifestation become one – inviting lasting joy and effortless success into your life.

Closing Section

Reflections: You Are the Shift

Over the last 21 days, you didn't just follow a process –
you became the process.

You showed up when it was hard.
You tapped when you didn't believe.
You wrote your truth even when your mind said, "What's the point?"

And now look at you.
You are softer... but stronger.
Clearer... but calmer.
Less reactive... more intentional.
Less "hoping"... more "knowing."

This is what real energetic transformation looks like.

It's not loud – it's rooted.
It's not about doing more – it's about becoming more aligned.
Take a breath and honour yourself.
You didn't just complete a ritual.
You initiated a new version of your life.

Continue the Practice: Beyond 21 Days

This journey was just the beginning.
Here's how you can keep the magic alive:
Revisit any day whenever you feel stuck, lost, or unsure.
Energy isn't linear – neither is healing.

Tap daily. Even for 5 minutes. Your nervous system remembers what safety feels like.

Keep writing to the Universe. Your relationship is real. Feed it.

Use your Intention Box. Every time you declare something, write it and drop it in. Let it be sacred.

Live as her. You don't need proof. You are the proof.

Let your life become a ritual.

Final Letter to the Universe

Dear Universe,

Thank you. For everything.

For the clarity, the chaos, the moments of alignment, and the moments that cracked me wide open.

Thank you for the 21 days of remembrance. For helping me come back home to myself.

I now walk as her – the version of me that already has it, already is it, already knows.

I'm not rushing. I'm not begging.

I'm aligned. I'm ready.

And I trust you completely.

With deep surrender and pure joy,

[Your Name]

Join the Brahma Muhurta Rituals Club

You've experienced the magic of early morning alignment.
Why stop now?

Join our Brahma Muhurta Rituals Club – a sacred online space where soul-led women gather to:

- Meditate and align at 4:30 AM daily
- Tap, journal, visualise, and set energy
- Stay connected to their power daily
- Rise in divine discipline, joy, and abundance

This is your soul tribe.
And it's waiting for you.

Stay Connected with Nisha

Let's stay in this energy.

Website: https://brahmamuhurtarituals.club/
Email: nisha@brahmamuhurtarituals.club

Scan the QR code to follow BMRC on social media and stay connected.

SCAN ME SCAN ME SCAN ME SCAN ME

I'd love to hear your story, your shifts, your magic.
Tag me, write to me, or send a voice note – I read everything.
Your story matters. And I'd be honored to walk beside you.

Final Words from the Author

Dear divine soul,

You've walked this path with courage and commitment.
As a mother, a seeker, a woman who has seen both silence and storm, I know what it means to rise without support, to pray in the dark, and to trust when there's no evidence.

This book is not a method. It's my heart.

It's my 4:30 AM breath.
It's my tears and triumphs and truth, transmuted into pages.
And if even one page cracked you open, If even one line helped you remember your power –
Then it was all worth it.

You are not here to chase life.
You are here to create it.

Walk boldly, speak gently, rise with grace.
We'll meet again – on a sunrise, in a whisper, or in a ritual.

With all my love,
Nisha Jain
Energy Mentor | Founder of Brahma Muhurta Rituals Club

Just 21 days changed your energy.
Now let your energy change
everything else....